Quarters

Books By James Harms

Modern Ocean
The Joy Addict
Quarters

Quarters

poems by
James Harms

Carnegie Mellon University Press
Pittsburgh 2001

Acknowledgments

Grateful acknowledgment is made to the editors of the following magazines, where some of these poems first appeared, occasionally in different form:

American Literary Review ("Fountain"), *Crazyhorse* ("Fable"), *Crab Orchard Review* ("Bluegrass"), *Denver Quarterly* ("Choose"), *Dickinsonian* ("Treasure"), *The Journal* ("Divorce"), *The Kenyon Review* ("Legacy," "Soon"), *Kestrel* ("Bruise," "Faith," "Laundromat," "Photo," "Votive"), *Luna* ("Now"), *The Missouri Review* ("Wire"), *Pleiades* ("Phonebooth"), *Poetry Northwest* ("Helicopter"), *Tamaqua* ("Dance").

"Soon" appeared in the anthology *The New Young American Poets,* edited by Kevin Prufer (Southern Illinois University Press).

The author would like to thank West Virginia University for a Senate Research Grant that was instrumental in the completion of this book, and the Eberly College of Arts and Sciences for its generosity and encouragement on many levels. Thanks also to the West Virginia Commission on the Arts for its support in the form of a Literature Fellowship, and to Linda Warren for her care and generosity in the design of this book.

Library of Congress Control Number 00-135218
ISBN 0-88748-352-6 Pbk.
Copyright ©2001 by James Harms
Cover and Text Design by Linda Warren

10 9 8 7 6 5 4 3 2 1

Contents

in every way for Paige...

...with light in my head
and you in my arms.

—*The Waterboys*

Money's not an abstraction; it's math
with consequences, and if it's a kind
of poetry, it's another inexact way,
like time, to measure some sorrow we can't
name....

—*William Matthews*

Quarters

Helicopter

Who are you
lifting the bag of groceries
from beside the tiny helicopter?
Your quarter didn't work,
your little boy expects
the blade to turn.
His hand is in yours
as you help him down
from the torn yellow seat;
its cushion makes a sound
so nearly silent, an exhalation.
You push the helicopter;
you kick it once,
then again. It doesn't move.
Oh well, you say, touching
his nose with yours.
He doesn't cry.
The pavement
is sticky with heat.
Cars exchange parking places
for the wide lanes between;
the street is marked down
the middle like a pattern,
the broken yellow line.
You enter the crosswalk
beside the mailbox,
pick your little boy up
beneath the arms
to let him drop a letter
in the blue throat.
And thinking it easier,
hoist him to your hip
and carry him across the street,
cars stopping to let you pass.
Then the helicopter starts.

It begins to hum, its blade
turning, the tiny carriage
lifting and dropping, pilotless,
flying. It goes and goes
as you walk toward Elm Street
where you stop for a second,
lower your boy to the sidewalk,
bend down to tie his shoe.
Then, hand in hand, you turn
the corner, the two of you, gone.
The helicopter rises and falls.
It is filled with quarters.

One

Legacy

Annemarie is nearly six. It is too early
in her life for the rain to remind her
of anyone, of a conversation that ends
in privacy, two people alone together
at a window blurred by warm breath,
by hours of sad talk, by the rain.

But she knows the crayons will run and smear,
that the butcher paper will turn to mud
if she leaves her art on the balcony
beside her slide, her plastic house.
Instead she's left a tooth in her meat loaf,
softly spitting a bite back to the plate,

knowing enough to mask her mouth demurely
with the napkin. Her smile is plainly
lacking when she lowers the veil,
though brighter somehow, like the one
grinning jack-o'-lantern on a porch
of carved snarls, the leering pumpkins

empty-headed and aglow, lit from within
like impressionable four-year-olds,
who follow Annie through sandboxes
and party games, pinning the tail
to Jeremy or Bruce; they follow her
anywhere, into the privacy of secret names

and imaginary friends, into trouble.
She is nearly six, though seven or eight
depending on the room, the age
of her playmates; she is always oldest.
And so her mother says, *Such a good tooth
for a seven-year-old,* then retrieves it

from the half-chewed bite. She rinses it
in the sink, hands it back to her little girl
and explains the tooth fairy, how she's different
from Snow White but just as pretty.
At the end of her prayers Annie shoves
the tooth beneath the pillow, finds a quarter

in the morning. *It's from fairy land,*
her daddy says, *a piece of moonlight*
for a pretty girl. Make sure you save it
for a dark night. Her mother waits for later,
when her husband's gone to work; she presses
the quarter in Annie's palm. *Don't worry*

about the nights, she says. Save it
for the rain, for that first remarkable rain
when you're alone, your hand in his,
the window a steamed mirror.
When he looks at you without listening,
when no one is listening: call me.

Divorce

Usually the bus from Phoenix was only
a few hours late, the grey dog on its side
"pursued to skinniness" down Highway 10
through Blythe and Joshua Tree, and perhaps
to exhaustion now and then, forced to lay up
in Indio to have its tires changed.
But once every few months he waited longer
than usual in Union Station, sharing ashtrays
with the homeless who borrowed cigarettes
and occasionally returned them when,
back again the next Saturday, he'd kill time
supplying lives for those entraining
to Oceanside or San Diego, sit and watch
them drag their rolling bags toward the tunnel
to the tracks or to the curb out front,
where the buses filled out the routes Amtrak
had given up. He'd smoke and drink a coke,
things his new wife forbid, maybe spend
some money on a coin-operated television,
the kind attached to a built-in chair
covered years ago in brown naugahyde.
He hoarded his quarters all week for this pleasure
since even a half-hour game show required six.
If his son was really late he might need twelve.
So when one night he let the TV go black
and looked up at the arrival board, the bus
from Phoenix now in when an hour ago
it had been delayed, his son nowhere
to be seen, he didn't worry. He called his
new wife, who hadn't heard from anyone,
then his ex-wife, who had forgotten to phone
to say their little boy would be staying put
this weekend, "Sorry." He hung up
and looked around. Larry approached him
for a cigarette, Lieutenant Larry who lived

nearby and carried his forty years in an army knapsack,
his favorite books in two bird cages.
He gave Larry his last Marlboro, then opened a pack
of Camels, all the newsstand had to offer
so late in the week. They talked about Las Vegas
and the years before the war, though he wasn't sure
which war, whether Larry was still Larry
or was speaking as his dad, which he did
on bad nights, Larry Sr. the drunk Colonel.
Then Larry saluted and walked away
toward the tunnel, where he slept sometimes
a few hours before heading home to the streets
of Los Angeles. "Angels," Larry told him once
as they watched a *Laverne and Shirley* rerun.
"This city's lousy with angels." He'd nodded
as if agreeing, though he didn't really care.
His son's bus had been late that night and he was
tired. And what the hell, angels seemed
as good a word as any for the vagabonds and bums
who fanned their feathers throughout the terminal.
"Yup," said Larry, "we're all angels waiting for wings.
Dead already, but waiting." He watched Larry's
back now until he disappeared down the tunnel.
His new wife knew he'd be late. His son was safe
in Phoenix, city of birds rising from ashes.
And he was an honorary angel as long as he stayed
put in Union Station, which by the look of things
(thirteen quarters and a few dimes) would be
an hour or so, a cop show or two sit coms,
four cigarettes and another coke.

Treasure

"Watch," she tells him.

They are a young couple looking out
a window at a garden, a path
of crushed shells. Beyond a lawn

of deep St. Augustine, poplars line
a redwood fence, they are
applauding…no—

their leaves are twisting
in a strong breeze
like hands wrung in worry.

A little girl appears
from the side of the house,
her white shoes on the white path;

she is carrying a trowel
in one hand, the other is a fist.
She drops the small shovel

and from the pocket
of her sun dress draws
a handkerchief, spreads it evenly

on the soil behind the forsythia.
Kneeling on the white lace,
she digs a small hole, big enough

for her fist. Whatever is held there
she buries. "What is she doing," he asks.
His wife smiles. It is a game to her.

"I just gave her a quarter."

Names

He scatters the four coins on the carpet.
At two he's learned to count, though on his way
to ten reverses nine and eight instead
of saying seven. Instead he tries to say

"nickel," a quarter in one hand, the dime
in the other. But he knows for sure the dull
brown disc is a penny, the coin that rhymes
with "funny," as in "Isn't she?" the fool

he laughs with while the rest of us just cringe.
"What's this!" she screams, "What's this!" holding up each
coin and cackling. Childless at fifty, unhinged
and frightened, she loves our boy, loves to teach

him what he knows: the shapes of money, its names;
and what we hope he'll never know, the shame.

Pride

He was on his way home from church
when he bent over to pick it up.
He heard laughter behind him
and turned: a little boy was watching
from a doorway, his head poking out.
He could tell there were other little boys
behind this one; their whispered laughs
were like a wind rising suddenly
along the gutter, stirring the leaves
and the scraps of litter. The little boy
pulled his head back into the vestibule's
oily shadows and the breeze of laughter
softened, though it remained brisk
enough to raise the collar of his coat,
cool the flush rising in his cheeks.
He knew better but he reached anyway
for the shiny quarter glued fast
to the sidewalk, watched without
looking as one, then three, then six
heads popped lose of the doorway's
soft darkness. And the wind broke
into a gale as he tried to peel the coin
off the cement, as he knelt and put
his whole body to the task, knowing
that for days he would be their victory,
a hapless stroller on a Sunday morning
on his knees in his best suit, trying
to make good on his good luck, the return
on his morning's investment of piety
and attention, how the priest had promised him
nothing in this life but hope, which even now,
his pride blown like a paper cup down
the street, was all he had.

Laundromat

She is too old to be playing jacks.
She takes threes, then fours,
then hears the dryer stop, watches
the clothes settle behind the round
window, her mother wheel the cart
across the busy laundromat,
bumping aside other, empty, carts.
The young man waiting with a basket
of white shirts leans forward
in his chair. The mother touches
her clothes, shuts the door, drops
another quarter in the slot. He sits back,
lifts a book, begins again to read.
The young woman takes fives and sixes.
It is afternoon, a room lit by
the long bars of late summer sunlight
through one wall of windows.
There is a liquor store next door.
A couple shares a can of beer
as they fold. Two palm trees
dusted with decades of smog
stand between the walkway out front
and the busy street beyond. Music
from passing cars bends as it falls
through the slightly ruined air.
The sound is so similar to the moans
of her grandmother—who hums
each evening as she draws her bath,
then sings with the skewed memory
of the recently deaf as she sponges
her arms and breasts—that she misses
her sevens and turns to look.
She is too old to be playing jacks.
Her face betrays the deep error.
She is surprised that no one is there.

Two

Photo

Jessica holds her canteen purse
like a last drink of water, the strap wrapped
around her wrist, her other hand in his.
Their first date falls on the last day
of summer, and he's exactly old enough
to be leaving soon for good,
his scalp shining through
his new haircut, his shoes
spit-polished for practice.
The Fun Zone is free
unless they want to play or ride
the Hurricane, lean out above
the sea and scream
as the old roller coaster strains
to hold the rails, as the car fills
with white chips of paint,
the wood struts shaking and shivering,
the burnish flaking off
at the end of another season.
In six years it will all be over,
the Fun Zone closed forever, the Hurricane
a pile of rotting two-by-fours slowly
softening to dust and salt,
a souvenir or two for the sad
and nostalgic who think it quaint
to keep a piece of wood,
maybe use it as a mantel
or carve a clock into the grain.
But Jessica wants a different
sort of keepsake. She pulls
the curtain closed, his face
next to hers in the little booth,
holds her cheek hard against his,
holds him still until the red light blinks
and the flash explodes and for a second

the light is all they are, the booth filled
with floating diamonds,
orange and yellow spots that aren't perceptible
in the strip of photographs
that drops from a slit in the wall.
But there they are, three times for a quarter:
Jessica and a boy she'll remember
like a ride on a rollercoaster, his haircut
new and too short, their faces fused
at the cheeks for as long as it takes
to stop time on the last day
of summer, 1967.
She keeps two of the snapshots, one
for her scrapbook, the other "just because."
He puts the third in his wallet.
"I'll look at it lots," he says
as they get in line again to ride the Hurricane.
She wants to scream, to feel
the wind pull her hair from its ribbons.
He just wants to kiss her in the air
above the sea as they take
the blind turn at the top,
where the whole world is there to see
if anyone's looking
though who would, the fast drop
just ahead and beyond that
the end of the ride: a platform
where they'll climb from the little car,
where someone else
will take their place

for as long as it takes
to get through line again, since what
they've decided to do
with the two dollars they have left
is ride.

Dance

A song shouldn't cost so much
she thinks as she feeds the jukebox
another dollar. But now what?
The whole roadhouse is waiting
for her selections, a dozen men
anxious to hear who she is, her friends
itching to dance, eager to prove
they don't care anymore
how it looks to close the circle
and sway together: three girls
on a Friday night looking for
nothing or no one, just a space
of clear floor between tables,
room for them to move and laugh
together as everyone looks
then looks away, muttering
through swallows of beer about
lesbos and maneaters.
She punches E-3, then M-11,
K-6, and finally B-7. She wants to end
with Springsteen, a slow dance
on suffering—who wouldn't?—
but the jukebox reads the alphabet,
starts with him instead, an old song
from *The River,* "Point Blank," B-7.
And her friends, who want to party,
to let the week dissolve in drinks
and their certainty in dance—
they just look at her.
They're not ready to throw
their arms around each other
and cry. "Bowie's next," she promises.
"'Let's Dance'." "Let's not," says one,
who slides a quarter across the table.
"Here's your refund on this one."

So they sit there and wait,
sipping their Seven-Sevens, until
all the shooting's done, until Bruce
has turned his back on another loss
and they can all get on with it,
which is what dancing is for,
with or without a man.

Bruise

Across the room behind the mirror
he slips a quarter in the slot.
She can't see him, doesn't want to, isn't interested
in being touched.
How are you? she says; it's what
she always says: safe and friendly, not really
a question. *What would you like to talk about?*
He doesn't answer, which isn't rare, not
unheard of, just dumb.
He drops a quarter in the slot.
She wraps a finger in a strand of hair.
My sister died of fever, she says, it's what
she always says, it sounds personal, like
she means it. *My mother healed herself
by baking bread for eight days straight,
until the racks of loaves reached the kitchen ceiling.*
He drops a quarter in the slot.
She has a bruise
the size of a knuckle below her collarbone
and she shows him, which she sometimes does,
though not often. Her husband pushed her there
on his way to work everyday,
on his way to poker, his way to bed.
He's been gone six years, she says, *but it won't go away.*
It's like a botched tattoo, a smudge of blue ink.
He says something, he says, *A tattoo is like a marriage.*
He taps the mirror with a coin.
She says, *How long were you married?*
She says, *Sometimes
I can hear the river from my bedroom window.
Sometimes it's the sea. But I know it's just the highway,
just traffic passing through.*
He drops a quarter in the slot.
She starts to say something else, how she's been to Hawaii.
She hears the door open, close.

Choose

When Auden saw the error in the bone
he turned to God. And now somewhere a man
can hear a fan turn air against itself,
a stunned and quiet evening, can hear the cars
and crickets, their senseless sawing
of pavement and forewing, can even hear
the early stars, their light sizzling through the leaves.
The woman he loves is deciding to let it live
or not. Neither boy nor girl, it is the size
of her thumb or a wedge of apple, it is
hardly real. In the bored blue afterglow
of an August day gone to ashes, she is
thinking of the years she has left;
she is doing the math. Yesterday he said,
"Why don't you just flip a quarter," and so
she left. And now the drone of starlight
and air conditioners, the man alone at the end
of his driveway, replacing the lid of an overstuffed
trash can, listening to an argument seep
from a window, turning this way:
a television; that way: a phone.

Faith

He drives her everywhere,
he drives her here. She tastes
sweet when they kiss,
like someone else. Like Cindy,
who tasted like a twist of licorice.
Back then there were sails
blown loose on the harbor,
rigging rattling the masts.
Torn nets awaited repair,
hung on poles, flecked with gill flesh;
scales spangled the docks.
There were cormorants
and pelicans arguing over buoys.
There were waves beyond the breakwater.
Back then his one knee or the other
was always an open sore,
he was always falling on the sand.
Cindy wore a white blouse patterned
with anchors. There was a carousel
on the pier. It was his first kiss,
he closed his eyes, he missed
her mouth, she tasted good.
He gave her cigarettes and chocolate.
In his mind he gave her
a lit match, a cup to keep it in.
And now she tastes like Cindy
but she isn't Cindy.
And now each friend whispers
something sour disguised as advice.
Each friend bequeaths to him
an apple core, a seed,
the root of a rose bush
torn from the arbor.
They want the best for him. They want
the best for him.

A sack of sticks has become
a heart. He is doing his best
though it isn't that much.
But there are coins carried softly
in a pocket, there to touch,
to rub between fingers.
There are coins.
Constancy. Faith.
One dime. One quarter.

votive

He had never been in a cathedral.
So when she placed the quarter in his palm
and closed his palm into a fist,
then led him past the wooden booths
to a row of candles beyond the first pew,
he looked for a slot to slide it in,
a knob to twist or an arm to pull.
He watched as she dropped her own coin
in a box then lit a long stick
by placing its charred end into one
of several hundred small flames.
The candles ascended in rows
like houses in a harbor town,
Lisbon or Nice, places he'd visited
without bothering with their churches,
preferring the shaded courtyards,
the walled gardens, a few small tables
topped with bowls of hibiscus blossoms
and baskets of bread, wine splashing
from the mouths of ceramic roosters
into square tumblers, tables surrounded
by sudden friends, the easy laughter
of the newly acquainted, the stories
near at hand for those who've never
heard them before. She had been
such a friend as he passed through
Puerto Vallarta. Yet here they were
on a Saturday afternoon in San Francisco,
where she'd shown up to visit him,
his own harbor town, the rain
thick and blowing like sheets on a line,
the avenues and alleys filled
with this falling laundry, driving them
up the wide steps into the cathedral.
She had shaken her head like a small

wet animal, blinding him
in another shower, so that they had laughed
into their hands, the sound suddenly muffled
like a door being shut on a busy street,
how the world becomes background
for the ideal of silence, which even
in a church is never perfected.
She pulled him playfully
through a second set of doors,
and even from there, fifty yards
or more from the alter, they could see
the small conflagration. "Mi madre,"
she said. "We must pray."
He knew nothing about her mother,
whether she was ill or dead.
And as he watched, she touched
the lighted stick to one of the smaller
candles in the bottom row, a fresh,
whole candle, unguttered and white.
She dropped her chin against
her chest, and for several seconds
her lips moved rapidly, until
she crossed herself and looked up,
as did he, to the figure of Mary
in a nearby window, her blue gown
flecked with red at the hem, her
son buried in the folds surrounding
her breasts. "Now you," she said
suddenly and forcefully, so that
he stepped forward and dropped

his quarter in the box without
thinking of a thing or a prayer.
He took her stick, relighting
it from one of the large candles
in the highest row, then ran it slowly
above the others, allowing their flames
to merge with his. And when he found
an unlit wick by hers in the bottom row,
a house nearest the harbor, he let the stick

stay there and burn, though he didn't
say a word; he kept the stick in place
until he was certain the candle was lit,
would burn for hours. And when
he lifted his head he saw she was
smiling. "Mi madre," she said,
her eyes reflecting back the many
candles, her eyes wet with rain,
he thought, or hope. Hope ignited
by faith. "Tu madre," he said.
And he turned back to his candle,
though by now it was lost in the tiers
of fire, which warmed his face,
warmed his hands when he held
them out, his clasped hands, a church
within a church. He noticed for the first time
how silent the flames were,
how very bright and silent.

Three

Fountain

Not coffee or a slice of pie, not a down payment
on a dollar, three of which will buy a sandwich
at the Sunshine Deli. She is bivouacked
on a concrete bench beside the fountain, surrounded
by bags and her collection of magazines,
some of which are for sale, though no one asks
for how much. Like other landscapes, this one
has a vanishing point, and she's it.
Even her language, laced with vowels rounded off
by meagerness, slips between its sounds, is lost
in the loose air surrounding an invisible friend,
with whom she's speaking, though with others
as well; it's difficult to tell. So when she asks
for money, the words make a wind that turns
each collar up, and blows the fountain spray
into faces, though it's *not* for coffee or beer,
not for pizza from Famous Ray's. "Please," she says.
"I need a quarter. I need a quarter to make a wish."

NOW

They waited for the music on the radio
to stop and it did, though somehow a few
seconds passed before they noticed,
much the way a day ends with a silvering
gone gray, darkness a hand on the shoulder,
a hug: it sits with you filling the room
with its silence. The message that followed
was meant to soothe as it shocked, like
the end of a fairy tale whispered
to a child at the edge of sleep: *Now.*
And even for them, enlisted to a duty
they were old enough to love, even they
felt the feather blows of a dream, that hush
of breath that arrives like a breeze
through a window, a dry kiss, the ghost
already closing the door behind him.
She retrieved the small pistol from its
velvet sack in the bread box. He
fit barrel to stock and oiled
his grandfather's rifle. There was time,
though quickly, to lick each other's
closed eyes, a ritual of sorts, his sweat
on her tongue, the bitter taste of mascara
across his gums, a cocaine freeze.
Offshore, beyond the breakwater,
the pirate station ended its broadcast
and released a single horn blast, as if
entering a slender bank of fog: a decorative
blast for a quickly passing vapor.
And what followed was the rumble
of a thousand shoes on concrete.
He paused to let the cat in as she filled its dish
an extra inch, enough for days or forever:
who knew? Simply put, the long wait was over.
And as they began to run with half the town

toward the harbor and the congregation site,
he saw the bright dome of the capitol
ignite with sunset, its copper tiles aflame.
And he remembered four children long ago
on the municipal beach, his brother's foot bandaged
in strands of jelly fish, one sister screaming
as the other continued digging, her plastic pail
filled with wet sand to drip into spires. The horizon
had seemed a botched watercolor of sun
over sea, a stain of orange that made the sky
a tissue torn with fire. He had run
for his mother with a joyful panic, knowing
his mission was of mercy, his brother's pain as vast
and distant as the execution of innocents
witnessed from afar, a television flickering
in a peaceful land. As now he ran with his wife,
the rifle easy in his arms, their pockets
jingling with keys and coins: skeletons,
quarters and dimes they would melt into bullets.

Gridlock

Even in Los Angeles the traffic eases up at noon, particu-
larly heading north toward Palmdale on a Wednesday,
since no one goes where there's nothing to do when
there's a chicken-salad sandwich nearby, the midweek
special at Barney's, coke and french fries included.

But something's wrong. The usual river-hum of cars on
the Hollywood Freeway has been hushed to a horn blast
now and then, the stream of traffic slowed to a standstill,
a twelve-mile-long parking lot. Someone rolls away his
window and leans out to see what's going on. Drivers
exchange looks, the *What's up* of raised eyebrows, shrugs
instead of smiles, though a few just shake their heads as
they inch their cars politely to the right, to the open
shoulder, the offramp just ahead: freedom. But there's
always one, in this case a battered Honda Civic, that
moves in fits and jerks, the driver beshaded and oblivi-
ous, cutting off the more cautious, his insurance long
lapsed. He's given the room he needs, the indignity of
a cracked windshield his red bandanna, a symbol of the
city's largest gang—not Bloods or Crips but the resigned
and dispirited, those who've given up and just drive.

The freeway has been closed at Melrose so the men from
Brinks can do their job. Red-faced and stoic, forced to
wear orange vests, they kneel and rise on the freeway's
sticky tarmac picking up over and over what seems to be
light, flecks of sun shining on the asphalt. Around them
it's just road and blue sky, the oleander and eucalyptus
audible in the new silence, California's ubiquitous wind
break whispering in a breeze, nearly laughing, though
really it's the motorists snaking up the ramp, pointing
and snickering, witness at the end of hours and miles of
traffic to this latest urban inanity: three men—the driver
and two guards—on their knees on the 101 northbound.

And of course, the road north leads to promise say the angels fleeing home: the fertile valleys near Modesto, the emerald forests of Marin. The road north is paved with hope for those tired of breathing ozone, of waking with trembles in a doorway, beneath a desk. The road north is littered with coins, dimes and quarters to be exact, for at last a truck has spilled money instead of oil, a bank's worth of loose change just beyond the temporary sign—FREEWAY CLOSED. Someone once said (perhaps it was Tom Hayden) that to solve all its problems L.A. should get its citizenry headed in one direction. But someone else (perhaps Tom Wolfe) answered with the literal and obvious: that if all of Los Angeles hit the roads at once there'd be a used car lot the size of Austria, a good idea he said, since then it would be easy enough to pave over the cars, the people, the whole damn city. But if all of Los Angeles heard there was money on the Hollywood Freeway they'd laugh it off as another empty promise—a call back for a sit com, an agent who loves the screenplay—though they might drive by for a look.

Tea

She arranged the interview months ago
    but now there is no where to sit,
        the table in front of them littered with cups

        and plastic cream containers, palomino
    spots of spilled coffee, a single bite
of pastry on a yellow plate.

But it's the only empty table in Seattle
    on a Saturday morning, so they sit down
        and wait for a waitress to clear.

        She's barely met him but believes
    they will have much to talk about;
she knows his songs, knows them like

the fairy tales her mother told
    to ease her into dreams.
        He has brought his baby daughter

        because he is "civilized with her around,"
    and he fixes the little girl's jumper,
which is sliding down one shoulder.

She wants to write this on her pad,
    to put the whole scene into words,
        but has decided against taking notes—

        "This is going to be an impressionistic piece,"
    she tells him, and he nods, leans forward,
curls himself around his little girl, a comma

enclosing a period. She commits
    the image and its tidy figure to memory.
        A waitress has recognized him

from across the room and is giving
the wrong table four lattes, rushing
to reach them, to clear their table.

"Tea?" she asks him, as she piles the refuse
on her tray. He nods, glances up.
"And a cup of warm milk," he says,

lifting the baby a little, "for her."
He looks at the waitress without
turning his head: his little girl has his

chin hairs in her fingers; she has his eyes as well,
which are the blue of Busch beer signs
shining in a liquor store window.

She nearly reaches for her notebook.
"What about you?" he asks her.
"Just coffee," she says.

The waitress smiles and moves away.
"I wish I could have coffee," he says.
Then he starts to hum, rocks his baby softly

in one arm, pulling a corner
of his dirty cardigan around her shoulders.
It sounds like a Leadbelly song.

When their waitress arrives
he puts a saucer over the cup of milk
then bobs his tea bag a few times.

"I used to drink 15 cups a day," he says,
nodding toward her coffee.
She starts to ask him about his stomach,

the lines in "Pennyroyal Tea"
("I'm on warm milk and laxatives, cherry flavored antacids"),
but he puts a finger to her lips, is dipping

his head toward his daughter, who is falling asleep.
He starts a soft song, "Jesus don't want me
for a sun beam," and she feels his finger,

still on her lips, drum gently as he sings.
On the table she notices a quarter, a portion
of the previous tip partly concealed

by a blue saucer, a yellow cup. She remembers
her mother's Fiesta Ware, the randomness
of dinners: a green bowl beside a cobalt plate,

a purple gravy boat, a persimmon serving dish,
how they faded and aged differently, no two
ever the same value or pitch, never the same

degree of black or blue. It was like perfect imperfection,
she thinks, and she wishes she could write this down.
He is finishing his lullaby, "Don't expect

me to cry, don't expect me to lie,
don't expect me to die for thee."
She sees that his daughter is more certainly

asleep than she herself had ever been
at the end of her mother's fairy tales.
He pulls his finger away.

"We'll have to do this some other time,"
he whispers, and she nods. He rises slowly,
careful not to wake the little girl.

"Can I use this?" he asks, sliding the quarter
off the table into his palm, "I need
to make a call." She can see a slip of wrist

as he reaches, as the sweater sleeve
pulls up his arm. And then he is
looking at her, eyes like larkspur, she thinks,

like the '68 Camaro her brother owned years ago,
metal flake blue and fast. It left a blur in the air
as it roared past.

Phonebooth

He is waiting. The rain has stopped.
The hood of his coat hangs behind his neck
in the shape of his head, like a sack
emptied of all but one potato.
She turns now and then to look at him,

her left hand in a fist at her ear,
the right a row of white knuckles
squeezing the phone receiver.
She is whispering with the force
of a child trying to extinguish candles

on a cake, as if he who waits
may know how she feels but not the words,
not the story exactly: she is having
a private conversation. But the booth
has no door, and he is waiting.

He leans against a parked car,
remembers the recent rain, pulls away
and feels the back of his trousers,
which angers him. She turns in time
to see him frown, his hand

dropping from the seat of his pants.
It begins to drizzle again and he pulls up
his hood. She can no longer see his face
when she turns once more to roll
her eyes; the receiver is making a noise,

a click that breaks the voice
she would rather not be listening to
into pieces, until a new voice
is asking for twenty-five cents.
She is holding her purse

between her ankles an inch or so
above the wet floor, and when she
bends to reach it the short
metal cord pulls the phone from
her cheek, so it swings loose

and slams against the glass wall.
Now she is struggling for her wallet,
is yelling toward the receiver, "Hold on!"
Some change spills out.
She sees his tennis shoes at the booth's

threshold, asphalt beyond, the patterned
metal floor, the thick Xs. His face
is still shadowed, it is still raining.
But in front of her own, just a few
inches from her nose—she can smell

the oil on his fingers, realizes
he is waiting to call for help,
a tow truck or some nearby friend
who understands engines—in a cupped hand
that barely pokes free of the frayed

and soiled sleeve of his jacket
is a quarter. "Here," he says.
And she takes it. She plucks it
from his palm like a thorn, trying not
to touch his skin. But of course

she does. And with the coin in her fingers
she watches his hand fold up, an anemone
in a tide pool. It is a fist
he puts in his pocket as he moves away,
as he turns to lean against the car, to wait.

Wire

A man walks out each morning on the wide sheet
of sand that shimmers into water to see if anyone
to see if she is bringing in the mail is part of the mail,
walks down the long rope of road to the highway,
the row of mailboxes, the names painted on tin,
walks out, he is walking out to carry home
the circulars, the bills for copper wire
and shells, the *Mojave Monthly*, a row of names
he hasn't heard aloud in years, he hasn't heard
his name in years, looks first as he would
in his shoes, scrapes out the scorpion, puts his hand
in the mail box, a tin coffee can, his name.

And then back, walks back, the work: the umbrella
glued to a stuffed raccoon standing on a giant spool,
wire running from legs and ears and tail to mirrors
scattered in the desert, mirrors wedged between rocks and clods
of dirt, a chair beside the spool, a switch soldered
to a quarter ("currency conducts current") and hooked
to the raccoon's throat. He sits, thumb on toggle,
answering each voice with a flick, sends a current
to seven mirrors in the sand, which hold the light as it passes
into water, the liquid surface of shadow, on/off,
on/off, he's waiting for her to hear him, how she said
to wait, he's waiting. And so a lizard feels a footstep,
the snake's long stomach sliding close. A lizard
just pretends to look away until the time is right and
it runs, it runs without its tail if you step on its tail
you can keep the tail, it runs, it knows. "You'll know,"
she said. He is certain he will know. She is not the concertina
of ribs he found bleached and ruined near the Stone of Visits.
She was taken away and she will return. She will.

Driving east from Barstow, the radio a storm of sand
and then it's him, speaking his history as frequency,

the blown history of a man in his trailer.
He is walking out on the wide water of sand,
the many ways of water, he places his hand on the raccoon's
back its stiff spine and he speaks into a can
strung to the coon's teeth. He says, "I hear you,
do you hear me? I hear you, do you hear me?"
He hands the air the can. It hears as well it hears
the sea as anyone would in a shell, the many ways of water.
He holds the can high to the desert wind, to the dust scraped
from the heavy sand, lets the desert answer the sea.
And as the wind rises it becomes a moan in the can.
And when he turns it just a little, the moan becomes a whistle.
He is calling her home.

Four

Moral

The father liked to make his points.
And so he set the checkerboard with coins,
quarters on his side, nickels for his son.
The rules were "same as always, though
winner takes all," and since they weren't
his nickels, the son said, "Sure."
And sure enough, his father's heavy
coins were quicker to jump the soft nickels,
so that soon the son was down to
twenty-five cents, twenty of that in kings.
His father reached suddenly and swept
the nickels from the board, replacing
them with a single quarter, indistinguishable
from the others snug in their black squares.
He looked across the table at his son,
smiled and raised his eyebrows.
And when he nodded solemnly the son
answered with a nod of his own, as if
the moral of this or any other story
was as clear as currency: the path
of coins in any wasted life begins
with a father's silver dollars and ends
in pennies. But it's the years of making
nickels into quarters that makes the man.
Or something.

Fable

He can't believe his luck. Just a block
from the beach a small Toyota pulls out
as he turns onto Ocean Avenue. He parks
in the tight space, zippering his car
between a Volvo and a tall truck,
unstraps the surfboard from the roof,
begins to unload the trunk: an icechest,
two towels, a wetsuit and some wax.
And then...what? A strange sound,
like a flag being planted in sand.
He looks up, sees the meter turning
over, the yellow warning sign
inching to red, a hiss like a spring
winding down. Before his hand
touches his pockets he knows
there's nothing there, no dimes
or clean nickels, no eight or nine
quarters, which is what he needs
for a morning of surfing.

He looks down Ocean at the line
of awnings and storefronts.
The first shop sells cinnamon rolls
and as he starts through the door he sees
a hand-lettered sign in the window—
NO CHANGE FOR METERS.

He buys a soda for ninety-seven cents,
gives the woman two dollars and asks
for a few extra quarters, his voice
rising an octave at the end of the sentence,
a casual request becoming a plea.
She says, Sorry, can't do it, points
at the register, another sign:
DO WE LOOK LIKE A BANK?!
He is about to say *Please* but she has turned away,

is spooning butter onto strips of dough.
He watches as she sprinkles cinnamon
and brown sugar, then begins to roll.
Outside, truants on skateboards
practice slides and strange hops.
They crash themselves on and off benches,
scarring the concrete and scaring an old lady,
who drops her bags, scattering frozen dinners
into the street. He watches a passing car crush
a chicken pot pie, then helps her collect
the rest. Perhaps she has change, he thinks,
but she *Can't breathe* she says, and sits down
on the sidewalk. He stands over her holding
her hand, listening to wheels crunch gravel,
the skaters hooting and laughing.
The old woman pulls herself up his arm
as though climbing a rope. She straightens
her hair, dusts the seat of her dress, walks
away across the street without a word,
though she appears to be crying.

The *Pollo Loco* is just opening for meals
of chicken parts and beans, egg burritoes
and espresso. The sign says SPECIAL
beside BREAKFAST, and below that
NO CHANGE. Further on the surf shop is leaking
boys from its open door. They're all shirtless
and tanned, skin brown as worn leather,
swim trunks huge and riding low,
arms and chests swarming with tattoos.
One has the word CHANGE in blue letters
on his shoulder, slashed diagonally with red,
a streetsign or warning: NO U-TURN,
NO EXIT, NO GUARDRAIL,
NO CHANGE. But it's CHANCE
not CHANGE, the name of a punk band
most likely, or how he sees the world,
his take on the next wave, Sartre
on a surfboard. Poorboy is inside

working the register, a friend from
way back, from a year of dawns
beside the pier. All those
mornings sharing waves, he's sure
to have some change. But it's
No way, man, won't happen.
He points at a video camera
in the corner. If the boss sees him
dispensing coin he'll lose his job.
Sorry, dude, he says, and shrugs.

Outside the day is brightening,
the fog lifting, an offshore wind
on the rise. He glances down an alley
at the ocean, at three-foot swells
as glassy as glaze on a sweet roll
peeling left to right from the getty.
He walks back toward his car,
stops to watch the cinnamon girl
check the oven. A boy strolls out
of *Pollo Loco,* half a burrito in his mouth.
He spills bits of salsa and egg
on his bare chest and flinches a little,
then jogs off. A meter maid
is making her way down the block.
He tries not to watch her, tries to hear
the clap of surf closing out, feel it shiver
the air around his naked legs.
He's left his board leaning against
the car, so the wax is starting to melt.
The meter maid is four spots down
writing a ticket. He's got two minutes tops.

Across the street the curtains part
on a tiny house, a crackerbox bungalow
from the 30's, no yard, a tar paper roof.
It's worth half a million in this market,
crowded on two sides by Frank Gehry
look alikes. The old woman waves

from the window; she seems to be smiling.
He moves toward his car, waves back
with one hand, fishes for keys with the other.
Hey, buddy, are you leaving? a guy yells
from a silver Ranchero, circa 1968,
surfboard in back. He nods, straps his own
to the roof, repacks the trunk, looks up:
the old lady is still waving.
And as he pulls out of the perfect
parking place, the door opens across the street.
She walks out and puts two fingers in her mouth,
whistles loud enough to stop time on Ocean Avenue.
And now she's waving again but this time
it's at her driveway, her long empty driveway.
She's waving him in.

Bluegrass

Bill Monroe, 1911-1996

"In life he had always passed out quarters to all
the children he saw. As he lay in the open coffin,
mourners—the grown-up children he had been kind
to—walked past one by one and laid quarters inside."

— *The New York Times*

How many find a way to make a word
their own, to bend it into slow silence.
How many find a name for who they are
outside the space of breath surrounding
Bruce or Bob or Bill?
                              In a small
community church of pine slats painted white,
a line of children has grown into baffled nicknames
for how they drive or play a banjo, for the way
a lock of hair curls, for a short fuse at the end
of Saturday night. A line of children grown taller
than mowed Kentucky grass baled and stacked
high enough to see Tennessee, a line of men and women
who've never left Rosine pushes through ghosts
from the Grand Ol' Opry,
                                        those toothless shades who flutter
like loose laundry in a strong wind, who carry
unstrung fiddles and busted mandolins and try
to sing from torn throats, whose ragged lungs
can't hold the air...
                              the grown children of Rosine
step past the wrack of Nashville to drop coins
in a coffin. And though it can't be so
they hear their names as they lean down,
how he always gave them quarters and sang
their lives, sang exactly who they were,
called them by their given names:
John, Lewis, Betty, Sam.

                    Not Speed or Twang
or Curlicue or Rage. They lay their change in the felt
beside his hands and listen, though there's not a ghost
in sight with wind enough to sing.
                                    But somewhere
a broken Philco plays on a sunken porch, a car radio
carries on, though the wreck is smoking,
the body crumpled behind the wheel.
                                    As if a few
notes swallowed hard long ago are now songs
sung from silence, like the sky at dusk, how it seems to lose
its blue to black.
                    The color of daylight has fallen
from heaven, has landed in the grass. The bruised blue grass.

Piper

Even when he had the money Toby didn't like to pay.
The ferry held three cars, four if all were foreign, and as
many bikes and strollers as could fit along the wooden
rails. And in his glass box the skipper would pull the
cable, blow once as the ferry left the slip, twice as it
approached, while a boy from the island with his eyes on
the wheel walked the deck in a slow circle, collecting a
dollar plus passengers from the cars, twenty-five cents a
head from everyone else. The crossing took five minutes,
seven or eight in traffic, and before the harbor was
dredged to let in the big boats, dolphins surfed the bow
wake, children leaning out over the rails, their laughter
rising and falling as the ferry quartered the rolling waves
that rose in V's behind the yachts heading for the restau-
rants on the peninsula, their owners weaving and waving
their drinks, driving blind but slow enough to be avoid-
ed. Toby would walk just ahead of the toll taker, who
flicked the rods on the metal change maker strapped
to his hip and did the numbers in his head, thinking
so hard sometimes his lips moved in the mantra of easy
math—a dollar a car, twenty-five cents for each passenger
except the driver—thinking so hard that he rarely looked
ahead. And if the ferry was full, he might not notice the
ghost out in front of him, a shadow torn loose of its body,
advancing slowly and out of reach, saving his quarter for
the arcade in the fun zone or a pack of gum, though that
wasn't the point. Toby just didn't like to pay. But one
summer afternoon, dressed only in bathing trunks, bare-
foot and broke, he let the toll taker catch him. "That'll
be a quarter," the boy said without looking up. And
when he didn't pay the boy said it differently: "Twenty-
five cents." Toby smiled, stretched out his arms palms
up, Jesus in jams. "I don't have it," he said. The toll
taker sighed and reached for his pocket, the frayed pad of
paper, pulled his pencil down from behind his ear to

write the name, this latest miscreant, to add it to the tabs of half the island. But before he could find the right page he heard a splash, then the cheers of children turned backward on the benches out front, no longer looking for mythic dolphins. He heard applause from the tourists who recognized an event when they saw one, though what they'd seen was Toby, who was now gone: a hole in the air at the end of a dive. A man in a car handed him a dollar and said," You're lucky I drove," as the rest of the ferry's passengers moved to the rear of the boat and, one by one, dove into the harbor.

Abstinence

In two or three minutes
the sun will be gone.
Joe has read the weather page:
the dawn and dusk calibrated
to the minute, the two high tides,
the temperature in Bakersfield
identical to Istanbul. For fifty cents
—two quarters or any other combination
of change excepting pennies—
he can buy the *Oceanside Sentinel*
and contain the day in figures,
wink at Bill across the table
as the coffee shop on the pier fills
with diners—usually the old
and vacationing who value
the early bird specials—wink and say,
"That's it, Bill, it's over.
Scratch another one up for God."
And sure enough the ocean beneath them
is black, though still blushing
a dusty pink near the horizon,
the light of day reduced to a thin line.
There's no sun in sight where just
a breath ago it clung like a drip
to the lip of earth. They lift their cups
of coffee, touch them lightly and toast.
And though Joe is certain when day
will begin again, he says so long
to Bill with a promise to meet at 6:46
the following morning, which will give them
ten minutes to find a seat in a booth,
to order coffee and rolls; he will have eggs
if it's Wednesday. And though
it's far away and invisible
from their perch at the wrong edge

of the continent, they will watch
the eastern sky above the Saddleback Range
and wait for the glow,
for their next chance to get it right.

Soon

He had always supposed he would die first,
before her, though he didn't think about it much.
It was like a secret learned and then forgotten,
a letter that hurts and is hidden away in a trunk.
But he had always assumed that one of many gifts
she would give him would be to bury him,
and that was that, though now and then,
as he cleaned her hair from a drain or
sliced an apple into wedges for lunch, placing
half on a yellow plate for her, eating the rest
as he stood reading her shopping list taped
to the refrigerator, now and then he thought
of how much harder it is to be left behind,
and for a while he'd feel an ache in his hands,
as if he were trying to hold onto something
too tightly. Twenty-five years ago she was already
twenty years younger than he, sitting outside
his office, her name on a sheet of paper tacked
to the door, her name with others, each listed
by the hour: it was always 3 o'clock with her,
always Wednesdays. And he loved her immediately,
though of course, he hadn't known it right away.
Perhaps one day, as she pulled her books from a bag
and began to ask a question, pointing at a line in a poem,
perhaps he thought of how much harder it would be for her,
perhaps he thought this before he'd ever kissed her,

before he noticed how her glance left a streak
on his cheek for days, as if her thoughts could touch,
could leave the small bruises love leaves early on.
But even then there was nothing he could do about it.
Once, years after, he awoke from a dream where
he had watched her from a stand of black oaks
as she dropped a daisy in his grave. And later,
still dreaming, he had circled in the air above their bed
as she tossed loosely in the sheets without him

like an empty cup blown with paper down the street;
she had been wearing a shirt he'd left dirty in the hamper.
She wrapped her arms around his pillow
as though it were a sack of stones, as though it held her
in place on the earth, kept her from rising to join him.
And when he drifted on her breath out the open window
he had reached to grab the curtains; he had wanted
to stay with her, though he was nothing then, a breeze,
his hands passing through the thin fabric like smoke
through a screen. And for the rest of the dream
he wandered through their town disrupting
leaves gathered in the gutters, cooling a hot cheek here
and there: a breeze. He never told her of his dream.
Sometimes he watched her from the porch as she stooped
and straightened in the small side garden.
He watched her pull the carrots from the earth,
how she shook them gently before dropping them
in the basket. She wore around her neck
a small woven sack on a string, and in it kept
a quarter: if ever far from home and stranded
she could call. But she was never far from home.
And the sack lifted away from her breast as she bent
to pull a weed; it swung back and forth
like a hypnotist's watch; she took it off only
to sleep. And when he awoke before her each morning
he thought of her alone in the empty house
tending to the three cats, winding the clocks,
the few things he now did, stacking logs
on the front porch each October, phoning for oil
when the furnace went cold, filling the feeder
by the kitchen door. And of course it hurt him

to imagine her alone, as it hurts him now
to imagine what becomes of those who go, or worse,
of those who stay behind as wind, as small eddies of air.
He gathers the laundry in piles, wonders where
she kept the bleach. He lifts the sash, lets in
a soft wind hoping for the smell of lilacs,
though it's early yet, only April. He will have to wait
for lilacs, and for whatever she planted in the garden.
It is too soon to know for sure what is there.

Notes

"Legacy" is for Caroline Mulry.

"Divorce" quotes from a line in the poem "The Flames" by Denis Johnson.

"Photo" is after the song "Jennifer Johnson and Me" by Shel Silverstein and Fred Koller.

"Bruise" is after a scene in the movie *Paris, Texas* by Wim Wenders.

"Tea" is inspired by Kurt Cobain.